Life Lessons in Prayer
*A 30-Day Prayer Journal
for Parent's Guide to Prayer*

by
Chandra Carroll

An Independent Published Book

Copyright

Life Lessons in Prayer
A 30-Day Prayer Journal for Parent's Guide to Prayer
Chandra Carroll

Copyright © 2024 Chandra Carroll All rights reserved.

This book contains materials protected under International and Federal Copyright Laws and Treaties. Any unauthorized reprint or use of this material is prohibited. No part of this book may be reproduced or transmitted in any form or by any means, electronic or mechanical, including photocopying, recording, or by any information storage and retrieval system without express written permission from the author.

Scriptures quoted in this book are cited from the Holy Bible, King James Version, published under Zondervan Publishing © 2024. The text of the King James Version is in the public domain and may be quoted freely and is conformable to the Edition of 1611.

Disclaimer:
Although the author has made every effort to ensure the information in this book was correct at press time, the author does not assume any liability to any party for any loss, damage, or disruption caused by errors or omissions, whether such errors or omissions result from negligence, accident, or any other cause.

ISBN: 9798325163456

This book is dedicated in loving memory of my sister, Simona Monique Seller, my number one cheerleader,

and my brother, John Paramore.

ACKNOWLEDGMENT

"Lord, I pray that as your spirit is leading me to write this book, that your people will be blessed. I pray that whoever is reading this book receives what it is that you want them to see, hear, comprehend, understand, and use it to partner with You on how to pray and cover their children in prayer."

Psalm 127: 3 - Children are a heritage from the Lord, offspring a reward from Him.

Psalm 68:9 - You gave abundant showers, O God; you refreshed your weary inheritance.

Isaiah 43:26 - Put me in remembrance; Let us contend together; State your case, that you may be acquitted.

In Jesus name, Amen.

INTRODUCTION

I am writing this prayer journal because children are our future. As parents and adults, we will be held accountable for what we did and didn't do for our children. Prayer is something we all should be doing daily, but not everyone knows how to pray.

Our children need us to have a prayer life. Every day we participate in work, conversations, meals, sleep, and even fun; but we must make prayer a priority. The Bible says, train up a child in the way that he should go and when he is old, he will not depart from it. I have three children, and I pray for them all the time. I started praying for them at a young age when I read a book on prayer. I started realizing that when I stopped praying, all hell would break loose. I also realized that when I kept praying, things got better. I knew that I needed to write this book and share the importance of prayer.

I am encouraging you if you are reading this book, please take your words more seriously and the conversations that you are having with your children. Conversations are important to God. We are all God's children. 2 Peter 3:9 says the Lord is patient and not willing that any should perish, but that all should come to repentance. As you start being careful with your words, others may get offended and desire to continue joking with you negatively. Even if we experience this, it is important to pay close attention to what people are saying daily. It is even more important to pay attention to the words we speak to our children.

Once I realized how powerful words are, I began to command my day. I understood that I have plans, but His plans are better. I would ask God to show me how to talk, help me with my job, and cancel all assignments sent to harm me and my children.

As you start your day, please begin to speak about your day. Allow Him to help you with that issue, adapt to that day, and work everything for your good. The principle of binding and losing is a method to forbid or permit the words that are released over our children's lives. Binding and losing is the transfer of authority from eternity into time. Believers can pray to access this power. As we are praying for our children, we must recognize the power and authority that we truly possess.

We must stay connected to God. We should strive to achieve, find purpose, learn to grow, solve problems, and focus on the reason we are here.

Even in our purpose for our children, we must understand that there is an assignment attached to their lives. Our goal must be to hear from God on how we help our children as well as others. We must always remember that people come into our life for two reasons, to make it better or worse.

Those that God has placed in our lives; He will show us through prayer. As you are praying for your children, hear God's still small voice leading and guiding you every step of the way.

DAY ONE

We all know that children are the future of the world, but the world is being controlled by so much darkness. We as adults are supposed to stand in the gap. There is a saying that if you don't stand for something you will fall for anything. There is another saying that says it takes a village to raise a child. Whether your village is your family, friends, or church; it is important to place our children in the center of our prayers.

Let's take a stand and pray for our children.

Prayer

"The Spirit of the Lord is here and where the Spirit of the Lord is there is liberty. I plead the blood over our children. I plead the blood over their minds. I speak to every spirit that would cause mental attacks. And I decree and declare that God is taking their thoughts back. I break the spirit of anxiety and fear. I rebuke every anxiety attack. And I decree and declare that the children of God are right now free. In Jesus name, Amen."

SCRIPTURE

Psalm 127:3 - Behold, children are a gift from the Lord, the fruit of the womb a reward.

DAY TWO

Genesis 1:27 says, "God created man in His own image, in the image of God He created him: male and female He created them." Let me give you a little background about God. God is a Spirit, meaning God does not have a body. That's the difference between us and God. Spirit is the non-physical part of a person. That's why our body is so important. The only way an entity can enter the world we live in is through a body.

Prayer

"Jesus, you have cast out the prince of this world. I bind the prince of the power of the air. I bind the principalities and powers in this region. I command every principality to eat its own words. For the weapons of our warfare are not carnal but they are mighty through God. For we don't war against flesh and blood but against principalities and powers. I cut off the assignment of confusion. I cut off the assignment of disruption in the name of Jesus. In Jesus name, Amen."

SCRIPTURE

John 1:14 - The Word became flesh and made his dwelling among us. We have seen his glory, the glory of the one and only Son, who came from the Father, full of grace and truth.

DAY THREE

It is important to completely comprehend the purpose of the heavenlies when it comes to your prayer life. The First Heaven is the heaven we see with our natural eyes. The Second Heaven is where Satan has his throne and the fallen angels dwell. The Third Heaven is where God has His throne and rules and reigns over the universe. Jesus Christ, after His death and resurrection, ascended to the heavenly places, which is defined as sitting at the right side of the throne. Things like God, the soul, thoughts, feelings, molecules, and atoms cannot be seen but they still exist. We must continue to believe and pray to God even though we cannot see Him.

Prayer

"Lord, we pray for your glory to shower down upon us. We speak to the heavenlies that line up with the Word of God and claim victory over our lives. Lord as it is in heaven, let it be here on earth. I declare an open heaven! In Jesus name, Amen."

SCRIPTURE

Psalms 19:1 - The heavens declare the glory of God; the skies proclaim the work of His hands.

DAY FOUR

We were created to love our neighbors, be caretakers created for good, and have a relationship with God. There is a movie that Denzel Washington plays in called Fallen. In the movie, he is trying to kill a man, but it is really a spirit. Just by touching a person, a spirit will transfer and take over the person's body. You see, Hollywood knows what is going on. They are telling us and showing us, but we are blind because people don't study or believe the words of the Bible. As we focus on protecting and covering our children, we must be mindful of the transference of spirits.

Prayer

"We eulogize that thing that attempted to take our kids out. And we pronounce it dead right now in the name of Jesus. We eulogize that spirit that tried to destroy their purpose. I speak that in our belly lies a yoke destroying anointing. The chain breaker is here. Every weapon that rises against our kids, I condemn. Every curse that rises against our kids, I condemn. In Jesus name, Amen."

SCRIPTURE

2 Timothy 2:15 - Study to show thyself approved unto God, a workman that does not need to be ashamed, rightly dividing the word of truth.

DAY FIVE

Prayer is the most important thing in life, but we don't use it like we should. No matter what, we all need help, and that help comes from prayer. Some people pray to the sun, moon, animals, mountains, trees, white magic, black magic, or even horoscopes.

This prayer is not the only source that can truly heal. Our source is Jesus Christ and He will always hear your prayers. Every opportunity that we have each day, we should pray for our children.

Prayer

"Satan, we send you a cease-and-desist order right now in the name of Jesus. From this day forward distractions, you will cease. Arguments will cease. Unmanaged emotions will cease. Spirit of rejection we cancel your voice. Spirit of confusion we cancel your voice. We muzzle your

sound. You will shut up in this season. And the God of peace shall crush Satan under our feet. In Jesus name, Amen."

SCRIPTURE

1 Thessalonians 5:16 - Rejoice always, pray without ceasing, give thanks in all circumstances; for this is the will of God in Christ Jesus for you.

DAY SIX

Ecclesiastes 3 says, "To everything, there is a season and a time for every purpose under the heaven. A time to be born, a time to die; a time to plant, a time to pluck up that which is planted; a time to kill, and a time to heal; a time to break down, and a time to build up; a time to weep, and a time to laugh; a time to mourn, and a time to dance; a time to cast away stones, and a time to gather stones together; a time to embrace, and a time to refrain from embracing; a time to get, and a time to lose; a time to keep, and a time to cast away; a time to rend, and a time to sow; a time to keep silent, and a time to speak; a time to love, and a time to hate; a time of war and a time of peace."

Prayer

"I release a prayer shield of protection around our children. I release every child's name into the atmosphere and declare that prayer warriors, intercessors, and prophetic watchmen are picking it up in the realm of the Spirit. I release that they shall not come down from their watchtowers until their assignment is complete. In Jesus name, Amen."

SCRIPTURE

James 5:16 - Confess your trespasses to one another, and pray for one another, that you may be healed. The effective fervent prayer of the righteous man avails much.

DAY SEVEN

Let me give you a little background about who God is. God is a spirit that does not necessitate embodiment. The spirit is not the physical part of a person, which is the emotions and character of the soul. The body is the physical structure of a person or animal in the bone, flesh, and organs. God does not have bones, flesh, or organs and that's the difference between Him and us here on earth. Our spirit is inside of our body and when a person dies it leaves the body. Death is an inevitable process that eventually occurs in all organisms at the end of life.

Prayer

"Lord, we know You specialize in our healing. You specialize in heart fixing. You specialize in mind regulating. So, I call on the heart fixer and I speak to every crevasse of the heart. I speak to the low place and call you to spring up in your destiny. I decree and declare that we have a sound mind. You have not given us the spirit of fear but of love, power, and a sound mind. In Jesus name, Amen."

SCRIPTURE

2 Corinthians 3:17 The Lord is the Spirit and where the Spirit of the Lord is there is liberty.

DAY EIGHT

We all admire someone or something who is influencing us and what is influencing our children is critical. We as parents should be our children's role models. God gave us a guide to use and that is the Bible. Bible means basic instruction before leaving Earth. You must stay focused. It's important to fast and pray. We must protect our peace. I was determined to keep my peace even if that meant leaving a friendship, job, or marriage. Pray for your peace of mind.

Prayer

"I speak to peace over every parent. I bind every stressful spirit. But we release hope in every doubtful place. We release peace in every chaotic place. We release birth in every barren place. We release fat in every wilderness place. We won't dwell in the wilderness. I decree and declare open rivers in every child! Out of your belly shall flow rivers of living water. Rivers of creativity, rivers of ideas, rivers of dreams, rivers of favor. Rivers of power. Rivers of strategy. Rivers of influence. In Jesus name, Amen."

SCRIPTURE

Isaiah 54:13 - All your children shall be taught by the Lord, and great shall be the peace of your children.

DAY NINE

Carefully watch your thoughts, for they become your words. Manage and watch your words, for they will become your actions. Consider and judge your actions, for they have become your habits. Acknowledge and watch your habits, for they shall become your values. Understand and embrace your values, for they become your destiny. – Gandhi

The brain and the mind are interconnected. The brain acts like a building, while the mind gives it life and decorates it. The brain structures every process, the mind is the expression of every thought, emotion, and experience. It is the mind that understands the spiritual. We must awaken the transformative power of our mind in the spirit.

Prayer

"Lord, I command every thought to be managed. I break down confusion. I break down delusions. I break down traumas. I break down triggers. No longer will we be held captive by our emotions. No longer will you be held captive by the past. No longer will you function on feelings. Our thoughts will be regulated in the presence of the Lord.

Identity, we call you forth. Confidence, we call you forth. Self-worth, we call you forth. Purpose, we call you forth. In Jesus name, Amen."

SCRIPTURE

Ephesians 6:4 - Fathers, do not provoke your children to anger by the way you treat them. Rather, bring them up with the discipline and instruction that comes from the Lord.

DAY TEN

Plant a thought and reap a word; plant a word and reap an action; plant an action and reap a character; plant a habit and reap a character; plant a character and reap a destiny. – Beckwaith

Prayer

"I decree and declare that our purpose was not canceled. For He knows the plans He has for us. Plans to give us hope. Plans to give us a future. Plans to give us blessings. Plans to blow our mind. Plans to open doors. Plans to shift our thinking. Plans to heal our heart. Plans to keep our mind. He has plans for us!

In Your presence there is clarity, and I speak that right now You're making Your plans clear. No weapon formed against us shall prosper. No weapon formed against our children. No weapon formed against our character. No weapon formed against our destiny. No weapon formed against our purpose shall be able to prosper. No unforgiveness will prosper. No depression will prosper. No anxiety will prosper in the name of Jesus. Amen."

SCRIPTURE

Proverbs 19:21 - There are many plans in a man's heart, but it is the purpose of the Lord that will stand.

DAY ELEVEN

An architect is a person who draws, designs, and plans. You see, God draws us first on paper and we are the blueprint of His creation. At first, we were not physical, then we became a living soul, being, and person. It's the breath of God that gives us life. God has always loved us and had plans for us.

Just like we as parents want and have great plans for our children.

Prayer

"We praise you God because what's in front of us is better than what's behind us. We praise You because we believe you just erased our entire past. We believe that your plans for us will be victorious. We believe your plans for our children will be great.

Your Word says every morning is brand new mercies. Every morning is a new season. Weeping may endure for a night, but joy comes in the morning. Our children will have joy. Every parent will have joy. We will follow your plans and purpose for our lives. In Jesus name, Amen."

SCRIPTURE

Jeremiah 29:11 - For I know the plans I have for you, declares the Lord, plans to prosper you and not to harm you, plans to give you hope and a future.

DAY TWELVE

As parents, we reflect on where our lives ended up and desire more for our children. As we pray for them, it must be our intention to focus our prayer targets on their purpose, destiny, and faith. Instilling in our children that they can be whatever they want to be is important. It gives them the faith to ask for God for anything. Remembering you can have what you say you can have will definitely open your world up to new possibilities. No matter what, be encouraged that even the crazy things in life work out for our good in the end.

Prayer

"We thank You, God for your purpose for our lives. We thank you for the purpose of our children's lives. Guide them oh Lord and order their steps. Teach them and watch over them with Your mighty hand. I speak over every child's life and decree that the Strong Tower is protecting them. You are the Strong Tower oh Lord. Hide our children in the safety of Your arms. In Jesus name, Amen."

SCRIPTURE

Romans 8:28 – For we know all things work together for our good who love the Lord, and who are called according to His purpose in glory.

DAY THIRTEEN

Healthy habits are important, and we all need to develop them. Parents should start praying and teaching their children how important healthy habits are. Finding healthy ways to eat and cook makes such a difference. When you eat better, you feel better. When you also change what you talk about and think about, your whole life gets better. Take the time to learn something new. I love learning new things and traveling. As you are learning, don't give up, just keep pushing. Add a daily routine and build awareness through paying attention to the words we speak to our kids. Replace the bad ones with good ones and use time management to pray for our kids.

Prayer

"I come in the name of the resurrected Jesus Christ. At that name, every knee shall bow, and tongue shall confess. I come in the volume of the book that is written for me. I am redeemed from the curse of the law. I am redeemed from the hand of the enemy. In Jesus name, Amen."

SCRIPTURE

Mark 11:24 - Therefore, I tell you, whatever you ask in prayer, believe that you have received it, and it will be yours.

DAY FOURTEEN

The blood of Jesus will speak for mercy on your behalf. It cleanses us from all sins. It provides redemption and speaks peace to the troubled heart. It allows us to enter boldly into God's presence. The power is activated when we speak Scripture. His blood called for mercy when He hung on the cross. If you are born again and have the blood applied to your life, then it speaks of better things for you.

The blood of Christ speaks. You can plead the Blood of Jesus over your children. As your children walk out the door, lay your hands on their heads.

Prayer

"I plead the blood over all children. I plead the blood over each child's life. I am redeemed and bought with a price. I break all generational curses of pride. I break all generational curses of rebellion. I break all curses and negative words that have ever been spoken over my life. I break all legal rights of all generational spirits to operate in my child's life. I break all curses on finances in my life. I break all curses of sickness and disease in my family. In Jesus name, Amen."

SCRIPTURE

Romans 8:26 - Likewise, the Spirit helps us in our weakness. For we do not know what to pray for, but the Spirit intercedes for us with groanings too deep for words.

DAY FIFTEEN

Identity is complex and ever-evolving. Identity influences our thoughts and decisions. Think about who you are in your personal traits. It encompasses our experiences, values, and relationships that create one's sense of self. We should pray for our children's identities. The enemy does not want us to know who we are in God.

Our specific appeals to Him demonstrate the urgency of God to move in our children's lives.

Prayer

"I break all oaths, all vows, all contracts with the devil from ancestors in the name of Jesus. The contract is broken. The contract is null and void. Satan you may have bruised the heel, but you should have crushed the head because now we can stand flat-footed and say that not another girl in my family will go through what my mom went through. Not another boy in my family will go through what my dad went through. My daughter, my niece, and my cousin won't go through this. The contract is broken. In Jesus name, Amen."

SCRIPTURE

Philippians 4:6 - Do not be anxious about anything, but in everything by prayer and supplication with thanksgiving let your requests be made known to God.

DAY SIXTEEN

Communication with God activates relationships, perpetuates promise, and dominates principalities. We hold the authority to precisely design a blueprint of instructions to orchestrate the plans and the purposes of God for our children and our families. What a responsibility and honor that He counted us worthy to lay before His throne and pursue Him in all certainty of His ability to deliver these plans according to His will.

Prayer

"I quench with the shield of faith every fiery dart of the enemy. I quench every fire of wickedness. I quench every fire of poverty. I quench every fire of fear. I quench every fire thrown at our children. The enemy will not burn up their harvest. The enemy will not burn up our harvest. For we are the seed of Abraham. We are seated in heavenly places. So, we take our position and bind principalities. We take our position and bind the works of darkness. We take our position and bind every enemy. In Jesus name, Amen.

SCRIPTURE

James 5:16 - Therefore, confess your sins to one another and pray for one another, that you may be healed. The prayer of a righteous person has great power as it is working.

DAY SEVENTEEN

The consistency of prayer conditions our spirit in a constant sensitivity. Our timetable is set on a definite moment of the day that has been allotted for our spirit-filled interaction with God. There He is awaiting our arrival each and every day, in great anticipation of the conversation that is to occur. When God shows up, we obtain the opportunity to enter into a daily covenant with God. This covenant places a stamp of guarantee that we have attained the dwelling place. We present God with a scheduled time to take up residency at this time.

Prayer

"Lord, we ask that you walk with our children. We know that you cover them. Hear us as we desire to have faith in the safety of our kids. Lord, we need to believe that you will make a way. I come against every spirit that will cause every parent to think negatively. I come against every spirit that will allow every parent to think they're alone. You're not in this by yourself. God is with you. I pray for the strength of every parent. In Jesus name, Amen."

SCRIPTURE

Colossians 4:2 - Continue steadfastly in prayer, being watchful in it with thanksgiving.

DAY EIGHTEEN

Possessing occupancy in an exact location signifies the spiritual residency that has been taken up in that place. Asking Him to occupy, influence, and invade our space delivers a summons of God to inhabit in this place. Our plea before the Lord must be for Him to live in us and dwell allowing our prayer closet to be infested with the presence of the Lord. Defining a regularly used area for prayer also creates territorial reign. Solidifying such a safe haven upholds recognition of the type of honor that He deserves in our discipline to cater to and grant God with a set place of reverence.

Prayer

"Speak Lord. Speak to our hearts. Speak to our spirit. Give us the consistency that we need. I pray that as we walk in discipline, we may receive direction. As we walk in discipline, we may receive clarity. I decree and declare a shift in thinking this week. Breathe on us a fresh wind of new thoughts. The wind of God is creating consistency. Wind of God blow. Blow on our children. In Jesus name, Amen."

SCRIPTURE

Matthew 6:6 - But when you pray, go into your room and shut the door and pray to your Father who is in secret. And your Father who sees in secret will reward you.

DAY NINETEEN

Prayer seeks to provide repentance to our souls, subjection to our bodies, sensitivity to our spirits, and vulnerability to our hearts. The purpose of our prayer should be led with a contrite heart and a broken spirit. Our purpose in prayer should be to speak the desires placed in our hearts by God and entertain His glory with words of humility, sincerity, and authority. Within each prayer, there should be such a purpose that restrains oneself from praying aimlessly. We hold the authority to precisely design a blueprint of instructions to orchestrate the plans and the purposes of God.

Prayer

"For you anoint our head with oil and our cup runs over. You anoint our hands with oil and we're able to war for our kids. You anoint our feet with oil and we're able to stand during trouble because you're fighting for us. We don't have to fight this battle. You didn't let us give up on our children. You didn't let us lose. I even pray for a second wind. Give us a second wind amid transition. We have faith in You. In Jesus name, Amen."

SCRIPTURE

Jeremiah 33:3 - Call unto me, and I will answer thee, and show thee great and mighty things, which thou knowest not.

DAY TWENTY

When praise precedes prayer, it eradicates all distractions, hindrances, and limits that may desire to alter the flow of the Spirit. God inhabits the praises of His people. As we approach the Lord with praise, we sound an alarm unto His ears that notifies God to embrace us as we speak wondrous praises unto His name. Praise destroys yokes, lifts heaviness, and binds strongholds that attempt to constrict our interaction with God. As we praise, we present a preamble to words released from our lips to God's heart.

Prayer

"Open up our ears to hear. Prick our hearts to hear you. Stir our spirits to hear you. We need to hear you, Lord. We need your presence. We need your spirit. We came into this season for a shift. We claim this season is the shift season. Shift us to a new level. Shift us into a new dimension. I come against all distractions, all decoys, all deception that attacks our children. I speak that in Your presence we highjack the atmosphere, so it doesn't affect our assignment. In Jesus name, Amen."

SCRIPTURE

Romans 12:12 - Rejoice in hope, be patient in tribulation, be constant in prayer.

DAY TWENTY-ONE

Making our petitions known unto God means revealing to Him what desires or needs we carry in our hearts. Rendering this entreaty to a God who is declaring unto us to ask of Him, is the pivotal portion of petitions in our prayer time. James 4:3 says that we ask and do not receive because you ask amiss. Our prayers should be created from strategically implementing these petitions as opposed to laying before God erroneous repetition. As you grow in God, this should strengthen your prayers along with specific petitions that according to His will, shall reflect His desires for the lives of our children.

Prayer

"I speak to the rooms that haven't been entered yet. I decree and declare that gifts are being prepared for platforms that I haven't been touched. This voice is being equipped for stages that haven't been stepped on. Help us manage the opportunity. We won't squander Your plans. We won't waste Your favor. We even thank You for the ingenuity of heaven. In Jesus name, Amen."

SCRIPTURE

Matthew 6:9 Pray then like this: Our Father in heaven, hallowed be your name. Your kingdom come, your will be done, on earth as it is in heaven. Give us this day our daily bread, and forgive us our debts, as we also have forgiven our debtors. And lead us not into temptation but deliver us from evil.

DAY TWENTY-TWO

Children today constantly attempt to compare themselves to their parents. There is a lack of respect and honor in the parent-child relationship. The child may even cast judgment on the parent in an unclear view of what the parent has dealt with in their life. Children are not experienced enough to place judgment on a parent, let alone to provide an opinion about their life. Their focus is the parent's resources that can be provided but would rather forgo the advice of the parent. There must be an improvement in honor and respect for each parent.

Prayer

"Father God in the name of Jesus I speak in authority and power to release your grace over our children. I come in the name of the resurrected Jesus Christ. At that Name, every knee shall bow and tongue shall confess. I come in the volume of the book that is written for me. I come to decree and declare. In Jesus name, Amen."

SCRIPTURE

Psalms 141:3 - Set a watch, O Lord, before my mouth; keep the door of lips.

DAY TWENTY-THREE

Children are always watching and searching for an example. As they watch closely, they begin to resemble what they see. It is a vital part of growing and learning. Having a proper example each and every day can provide children with a strong foundation.

Being able to see a visible representation of success, self-worth, and strength are great opportunities for children to mature into healthy adults.

Prayer

"Lord, I pray right now for our children. I claim victory over their lives. They are redeemed from the curse of the law. They are redeemed from the hand of the enemy. They are redeemed and bought with a price. I break all generational curses of pride. I break all generational curses of rebellion. I break all generational curses of poverty. I break all generational curses of addiction. I break all curses and negative words that have ever been spoken over their life. In Jesus name, Amen."

SCRIPTURE

Proverbs 18:21 Death and life is in the power of the tongue, and they that love it shall eat the fruit thereof.

DAY TWENTY-FOUR

Children today are not accustomed to authority. Authority is so unreal today for children. They are using profanity and disrespect towards our parents. Fighting their elders is not looked upon as inappropriate. It is our prayer that the honor be put back in place for adults in the lives of our children.

Prayer

"Lord, I pray that you cover our children in their sleep. Give them rest and give them protection over their mind. I come against any spirit at night. They will not be afraid of the arrow that flies by day or the terror that flies by night. I bind any attack on their life. I take authority over every demon that is released. I bind and take authority over all nightmares and demonic dreams. They will rest at night. They will be at peace. And the peace of God which surpasseth all understanding will guard your heart and mind. He's guarding. He's healing. He's breaking. In Jesus name, Amen".

SCRIPTURE

Proverbs 15:1 - A soft answer turns away wrath, but grievous words stir up anger.

DAY TWENTY-FIVE

Children, when they are young, they lay on your lap and when they are old, they lay on your heart. This is a saying that I learned from my grandmother. It is our job to love our children as parents. Sometimes we take this a step further and we begin to spoil our children. When this occurs, they really don't gain the opportunity to understand some of life's lessons. We as parents must pray and teach our children to pay close attention to their words and life choices.

Prayer

"I command all generational spirits that came in the womb to come out in the name of Jesus. I command all spirits of witchcraft from ancestors to come out in the name of Jesus. I command all pride inherited to come out in the name of Jesus. I command all rejection inherited to come out in the name of Jesus. I command all anger inherited to come out in the name of Jesus. In Jesus name, Amen."

SCRIPTURE

Ephesians 4:26 - Be angry and sin not; let not the sun go down on your wrath.

DAY TWENTY-SIX

As one engages in prayer, coming before the Lord with a heartfelt plea of forgiveness is pertinent. Asking the Lord for forgiveness places you in a state of humility, realizing that we are undeserving of His mercy.

Purifying oneself through forgiveness allows one to be presented without spot or wrinkle as you lay at God's feet. David asked the Lord to give me a clean heart and renew the right spirit within me. Purge me with hyssop and wash me white as snow.

Prayer

"Lord, we receive your blessings. Command your blessings over our lives. Release a blessing of heaven. Release the blessing of the womb. Release the blessing of Abraham. Lord we're knocking and doors of blessings are open to us. We're running and doors of blessings are open to us. We're seeking and doors of blessings are open to us. In Jesus name, Amen."

SCRIPTURE

Psalms 139:23 - Search me, Oh God, and know my heart; try me and know my thoughts. And see if there be any wicked way in me and lead me in the way everlasting.

DAY TWENTY-SEVEN

Our confessions to God should be one of honesty and transparency. Always mentioning sins that were committed unknowingly places just as much importance as sins committed knowingly. Psalms 139:23 asks. the Lord, "Search me, O God, and know my heart: try me, and know my thoughts: And see if there be any wicked way in me and lead me in the way everlasting.

Confessing your sins unto God leaves no room for disdain but opens the door for His undying love awarded to us. As we release our confessions, we simultaneously receive the right to pray on holy ground.

Prayer

"I break all assignments of the enemy against our strength in the name of Jesus. I break all spirits of the cankerworm, palmerworm, caterpillar, and locust in the name of Jesus. For God will restore the years in the name of Jesus. You will write again. You will sing again. You will smile again. You will create again. In Jesus name, Amen."

SCRIPTURE

John 1:9 - If we confess our sins, He is faithful and just forgive us our sins and to cleanse us from all unrighteousness.

DAY TWENTY-EIGHT

The Bible declares that we should enter His gates with thanksgiving. The word thanksgiving means to totally reverence through optimal gratitude to demonstrate one's appreciation towards God. There are many things to be thankful for and the bible recognizes the main things. Ephesians 5:20 "Giving thanks always for all things unto God and the Father in the name of our Lord Jesus Christ."

Prayer

"We thank you that what's in front of you is better than what's behind you. We thank you that God's about to bless your entire family. We thank you that God just erased your entire past. He said every morning is brand new mercies. Every morning is a clean slate. Every morning is a new season. Weeping may endure for a night, but joy comes in the morning. Wake up, it's morning time. Brand new. Brand new mind. Brand new thinking. Brand new heart. In Jesus name, Amen."

SCRIPTURE

Ephesians 6:18 - Praying at all times in the Spirit, with all prayer and supplication. To that end keep alert with all perseverance, making supplication for all the saints.

DAY TWENTY-NINE

When we understand the authority of the Word and the position of the Word in our lives, it follows that we have to pray the Word. The following are some reasons why we should pray the Word. God introduces His will in the Word. When we pray the Word, we pray the will of God and when we pray according to the will of God, the Word says our prayers will be answered. (1 John 5:14-15) Secular books provide knowledge and insight, but it is only when we read the Word that you come to faith. When we pray the Word, faith increases in our hearts. (Rom.10:17) The Word/Scripture reveals God's priorities.

Prayer

"Satan, we send you a cease-and-desist order right now in the name of Jesus. From this day forward distractions you will cease. Spirit of rejection we cancel your voice. Spirit of comparison we cancel your voice. We muzzle your sound. And the peace of God shall crush Satan under our feet. Rejection be crushed. Depression be crushed. In Jesus name, Amen.

SCRIPTURE

Philippians 4:6 - Do not be anxious about anything, but in everything, by prayer and petition, with thanksgiving, present your request to God.

DAY THIRTY

When we pray according to the Word, we learn what these priorities are and then we will be able to adapt our lives according to these priorities. The Word has authority.

When God the Father created the universe, He did it through His Son, the Word. The Word spoke a word and there was light and life and people and heavenly bodies. When we proclaim the Word, it becomes a declaration in the spiritual kingdom – the Word still has the same power. The Word teaches us about. When we understand God better, we can pray with more faith. Faith is as strong as the person in whom you believe.

Prayer

"I thank you for a week of miracles. A week of peace. A week of favor. I release that a prayer shield will form a hedge of protection around us and hide us from familiar spirits. I release names into the atmosphere and declare that prayer warriors, intercessors, and prophetic watchmen are picking it up in the realm of the Spirit. In Jesus name, Amen."

SCRIPTURE

1 John 5:14 - This is the confidence we have in approaching God; that if we ask anything according to His will, He hears us.

AFFIRMATIONS

I will have a great day. I will be productive.

I will learn something new.

I will learn from this experience.

I have a Helper to help me.

I have a great Teacher to teach me.

I am blessed. I am smart.

I am successful.

I am more than a conqueror.

I can do all things through Christ.

I will get through this.

I will win.

TESTIMONY 1

Let me give you a testimony about my daughter. She was experiencing kidney complications, and they began to shut down. This meant that she would need immediate medical attention, but I would need to provide my insurance. Social services reported that I did not qualify for Medicaid and therefore she would not receive the needed care or medication that she required. I began to pray and ask God to move on my daughter's behalf. After being in prayer, I received a call informing me that my health insurance would cover her medical needs due to my new full-time position. I started crying tears of joy. Look at God. When one door closes, He opens another door.

TESTIMONY 2

My daughter was 3 years old when she fell out and had to be rushed to the hospital.

When I arrived at the hospital, my daughter was not conscious and had not woken up. I immediately began to pray and petition God to heal my daughter. When the doctor took me to her bed, I touched her, and she jumped into my arms calling out my name. The doctor didn't know what was wrong and had never experienced anything like this before. They began to run tests and she even had to proceed with monthly checkups to ensure there was no brain damage. Again, I began to go before the Lord in prayer. I rebuked all distractions and stayed focused on God.

It is important when something happens that we stop going to people and start going to God in prayer.

TESTIMONY 3

Many people don't understand that children are a gift from God. Some people desire children but cannot have them.

I remember crying one day about something that my kids did that really upset me. I started praying and asking God what I should do. The Lord stepped in and began to give me Scriptures to write down. I went to Isaiah 43. God spoke this Scripture and shared with me that when we are upset at our children, this is how He feels when He is upset at His children.

I am giving this example because God has always showed up for me. No matter what mistakes we make, we are His children. He will always love us, and we should always pray.

PRAYER FOR PROTECTION

In the name Lord Jesus, Heavenly Father, I bow in worship and praise before You. I cover myself and my children with the blood of Jesus Christ and claim protection of the blood for my family, my finances, my home, my spirit, soul, and body. I surrender myself completely in every area of my life to You. I take a stand against all the works of the devil, that would try to hinder me and my family from best serving You. I address myself only to the true and living God, who has power and control over everything. Satan, I command you and your demon forces of darkness, in the name Lord Jesus to leave my presence. I bring the blood of Jesus between the devil and my family, my home, my finances, my spirit, soul, and body. I declare, therefore, that Satan and his wicked spirits are subject to me in the name Lord Jesus. Furthermore, in my children's lives today, I destroy and tear down all the strongholds of the devil against their minds and surrender my mind to you, blessed Holy Spirit. In Jesus name, Amen.

SCRIPTURES TO MEDITATE ON

Galatians 6:6

Philippians 4:6

Ephesians 4:26

Hebrews 10:19

1 Peter 2:24

Ephesians 1:7

Colossians 1:20

John 14:22

Romans 12:2

1 Corinthians 2:16

Philippians 2:5

Hebrews 8:10

1 Peter 1:13

Isaiah 26:3

Colossians 3:2

PRAYER FOR IDENTITY

I affirm Heavenly Father, that you have not given me the spirit of fear but of power, and of love, and of a sound mind II Tim 1:7. Therefore, I resist the spirit of fear in the name Lord Jesus, the Son of the living God, and I refuse to doubt or worry because I have authority power over all the power of the enemy; and nothing by means shall hurt me Luke 10:19. I decree and declare that I am a new creation. I am complete in Him. I am God's masterpiece. I am a child of God. I am righteous. I am dearly loved by God. I claim complete and absolute victory over the forces of darkness in the name Lord Jesus and I bind all the works of the devil, and cast them into the sea, in the name Lord Jesus. I cancel every assignment sent to harm me and my children this day in the name Lord Jesus. Amen.

Ephesians 2:10

1 Peter 2:9

Romans 8:2

Matthew 5:44

Psalms 110:1

Acts 20:35

Psalms 118

PRAYER OVER THE ENEMY

I release the Holy Spirit to bring God's peace, joy, prosperity, and total debt cancellation in the name Lord Jesus to my household and every member of my family for the glory of God and by faith I call it done. I break and smash the strongholds of Satan formed against my emotion today and I give my emotion to You Lord Jesus. I destroy the strongholds of Satan against my body today and I give my body to You Lord Jesus realizing that I am the temple of the Holy Spirit (1 Cor 3:16 and 1 Cor 6:19-20). Again, I cover myself and my children with the blood of Jesus and pray that Holy Ghost would bring all the work of the crucifixion, and all the ascension of the Lord Jesus into my life today. I surrender my life and possessions to You. I refuse to fear, worry, or be discouraged in the name Lord Jesus. I will not hate, envy, or show any type of bitterness toward anyone, but I will love with the love that God shed abroad in my heart by the Holy Ghost. In Jesus name, Amen.

3 John 2

Mark 11:24

Romans 4:3

Psalms 145

1 Corinthians 3:16

Luke 10:19

PRAYER FOR HELP

I pray for God's help to overflow our life. I claim that we have purpose and have obtained mercy finding grace in time of need. I place our prayer petitions before the Lord and seal them with the Blood. Open my eyes and show me all areas of my life that do not please you and help me to exercise your strength, grace, and wisdom to remove any sin or weight that would prevent our close fellowship. Lord, I need your help and guidance. I speak of the supernatural ability to overcome. Work in me to cleanse me from a ground that would give the devil a foothold against me. I claim the victory of the cross in every area of my children's life and overall satanic forces in the name Lord Jesus. I pray in the name Lord Jesus with thanksgiving, believing that I will receive when I pray, and I welcome all the ministry of the Holy Spirit. In Jesus name, Amen.

Isaiah 43:26

Isaiah 55:11

Psalms 118:34

Psalms 28:7

Psalms 34:4

Philippians 4:13

2 Timothy 1:7

THANK YOU

First, my Lord and Savior Jesus Christ receive all the glory. I want to acknowledge my kids, my mother, Jacqueline Young, Linda Gregory, and Christina Blake who always encourage me.

I also want to thank Janice Hunter for the prophetic teachings. Thank you, Yolanda Mercer, for being so patient with me.

I could not have learned what I know had Yarnetta Peebles and her sister Alice not encouraged me to stay in Apostle Betty Peebles' classes for 4 years. Bishop Joel Peebles, Sr. thank you for the spiritual knowledge of God's word in over 20 years of service.

I would also love to thank Rochelle Smith, Linda Montgomery, Lakeisha Smith, Pastor J.J. Hairston, and Pastor Trina Hairston.

Thank you, Malika Staar of MaliStaar Publishing, for helping complete this project at the drop of a dime.

And finally, I thank you, the reader, for your support on this project. I appreciate all your support.

ABOUT THE AUTHOR

Chandra Carroll is a God-fearing born-again Christian and mother of three children. She has her diploma in Discipleship along with ministry classes. Chandra has a passion for speaking the Word of God to people. She loves to pray for people. Her hobbies include spending time with her family, and five grandchildren. She loves traveling, music, skating, dancing, and singing.

For more information or speaking engagements, contact Chandra at carrollchandra07@gmail.com.

Made in the USA
Middletown, DE
26 March 2025